The
Cybersecurity
Mindset

Neil King

Table Of Contents

Chapter 3: The Cybersecurity Mindset

The importance of cultivating a cybersecurity mindset

Understanding the psychology of cyber attackers

Steps to develop a cybersecurity culture in the workplace

Integrating cybersecurity into business strategy

Chapter 4: Data Privacy and Protection

Understanding data privacy and protection

The importance of data privacy regulations

Best practices for protecting sensitive data

Tools and technologies for data protection

Chapter 5: Cyber Threat Intelligence

Understanding cyber threat intelligence

The importance of threat intelligence in cybersecurity

How to collect and analyze threat intelligence

Tools and technologies for threat intelligence

Chapter 6: Cybersecurity Compliance and Regulation

Understanding cybersecurity compliance and regulation

Overview of cybersecurity regulations around the world

Best practices for compliance and regulation

Tools and technologies for compliance and regulation

Chapter 7: The Future of Cybersecurity

Emerging cybersecurity trends

The impact of artificial intelligence and machine learning on cybersecurity

The role of cybersecurity in digital transformation

Future challenges and opportunities in cybersecurity

Chapter 8: Conclusion

Summary of key takeaways

Final thoughts on cultivating a culture of vigilance

Call to action for readers to take steps to improve their cybersecurity mindset.

Chapter 1: Introduction

Importance of cybersecurity in today's world

In today's world, the importance of cybersecurity cannot be overstated. As technology continues to advance at an unprecedented pace, businesses and individuals alike are increasingly vulnerable to cyber attacks. From data breaches to ransomware attacks, cyber threats are becoming more sophisticated and more frequent, making cybersecurity an essential aspect of modern life.

One of the most significant benefits of cybersecurity is the protection of sensitive information. With the vast amount of data that is stored online, it is crucial to ensure that this data remains secure and confidential. Businesses that fail to implement adequate cybersecurity measures risk losing valuable information, which can have severe consequences for their reputation and bottom line.

Another important aspect of cybersecurity is the prevention of cybercrime. Cyber threats can take many forms, from phishing scams to malware attacks, and they can have devastating effects on both businesses and individuals. By investing in cybersecurity measures such as firewalls, antivirus software, and intrusion detection systems, organizations can reduce the risk of cyber attacks and protect themselves against potential losses.

In addition to protecting against cybercrime, cybersecurity is also essential for compliance and regulation. Many industries are subject to strict regulations around data privacy and protection, and failure to comply with these regulations can result in significant fines and legal penalties. By implementing cybersecurity measures, businesses can ensure that they are meeting these regulations and avoiding any potential legal issues.

Finally, cybersecurity is essential for maintaining trust and confidence in technology. As more and more of our lives move online, it is essential that we can trust the technology that we use. By investing in cybersecurity measures, businesses can demonstrate that they take the security of their customers' data seriously, and can build trust and confidence in their brand.

Overall, it is clear that cybersecurity is an essential aspect of modern life. By investing in cybersecurity measures, businesses and individuals can protect themselves against cyber threats, comply with regulations, and maintain trust and confidence in technology. As technology continues to advance, it is essential that we prioritize cybersecurity to ensure a safe and secure future for all.

Overview of the book's content

The Cybersecurity Mindset: Cultivating a Culture of Vigilance is a comprehensive guide that explores the complex world of cybersecurity and the importance of cultivating a culture of vigilance in today's technology-driven world. This book is aimed at a trade audience interested in technology and business and the future of the world with specific niches in cybersecurity, data privacy and protection, cyber threat intelligence, cybersecurity compliance, and regulation.

The book provides an overview of the current state of cybersecurity and the various threats that organizations and individuals face. It explores the different types of cyber attacks, such as phishing, malware, ransomware, and social engineering, and provides practical advice on how to protect against them.

In addition, the book offers insights into the importance of data privacy and protection, and the steps organizations can take to ensure their data is secure. It also delves into the world of cyber threat intelligence, providing an overview of the different types of threat intelligence and how organizations can use it to identify and mitigate cyber threats.

The book also covers the complex world of cybersecurity compliance and regulation, providing an overview of the different regulations that organizations need to comply with, such as the General Data Protection Regulation (GDPR) and the Cybersecurity Information Sharing Act (CISA). It also provides practical advice on how to comply with these regulations and avoid penalties.

Throughout the book, the authors emphasize the importance of cultivating a culture of vigilance within organizations. This involves educating employees about the importance of cybersecurity, providing them with the tools and resources they need to protect themselves and the organization, and creating a culture of accountability where everyone takes responsibility for cybersecurity.

Overall, The Cybersecurity Mindset: Cultivating a Culture of Vigilance is an essential resource for anyone interested in cybersecurity, data privacy and protection, cyber threat intelligence, cybersecurity compliance, and regulation. It offers practical advice and insights that can help organizations and individuals protect themselves against cyber threats and cultivate a culture of vigilance.

Target audience and their needs

Target audience and their needs

To effectively cultivate a culture of vigilance around cybersecurity, it is important to understand the target audience and their needs. This includes both individuals and organizations who are interested in technology and business, as well as those who are concerned about the future of the world. The following sub-sections will explore the specific needs of different niches within the cybersecurity industry, including data privacy and protection, cyber threat intelligence, cybersecurity compliance and regulation.

Data Privacy and Protection

Individuals and organizations that are concerned with data privacy and protection need to be able to trust that their personal and sensitive information is secure. This includes everything from financial data to medical records to personal identification information. Cybersecurity professionals must be able to provide secure solutions for data storage and transmission, as well as be able to detect and respond to any breaches that occur.

Cyber Threat Intelligence

For those in the cybersecurity industry who are focused on cyber threat intelligence, it is important to have a deep understanding of the latest trends and tactics used by cyber criminals. This includes staying up-to-date on the latest malware and hacking techniques, as well as being able to analyze data to identify potential vulnerabilities within an organization. Cyber threat intelligence professionals must also be able to communicate effectively with other security professionals and executives to ensure that everyone is on the same page when it comes to protecting the organization.

Cybersecurity Compliance and Regulation

Finally, those in the cybersecurity industry who are focused on compliance and regulation need to be able to navigate the complex world of laws and regulations around data protection. This includes understanding the various requirements around data privacy, as well as being able to implement policies and procedures that comply with these regulations. Cybersecurity compliance and regulation professionals must also be able to stay up-to-date on changes to these laws and regulations, and ensure that their organization is always in compliance.

In conclusion, understanding the specific needs of different niches within the cybersecurity industry is crucial for building a culture of vigilance around cybersecurity. Whether you are focused on data privacy and protection, cyber threat intelligence, or cybersecurity compliance and regulation, it is important to stay up-to-date on the latest trends and techniques in order to effectively protect your organization. By working together and sharing knowledge, we can build a safer and more secure cyber landscape for everyone.

Chapter 2: Cybersecurity: What You Need to Know

Understanding cyber threats and attacks

The world is becoming increasingly interconnected thanks to the rapid advancements in technology. However, this interconnectivity has also brought with it a host of threats and risks that have the potential to disrupt businesses and individuals alike. Cyber threats and attacks have become a major concern for organizations of all sizes, as they have the potential to cause significant financial losses, damage reputations, and compromise sensitive data.

Understanding the various types of cyber threats and attacks is essential for any organization that wants to protect itself from these risks. There are a wide variety of cyber threats and attacks that can impact businesses, including malware, phishing, ransomware, and denial-of-service attacks. Each of these types of attacks has its own unique characteristics and can cause significant harm to organizations that are not adequately prepared.

Malware is a type of software that is designed to damage, disrupt, or gain unauthorized access to a computer system. Malware can take many different forms, including viruses, worms, Trojan horses, and spyware. Phishing attacks are a type of social engineering attack that uses email or other communication channels to trick individuals into divulging sensitive information such as passwords or credit card numbers.

Ransomware is another type of malware that has become increasingly common in recent years. This type of malware encrypts an organization's data and demands a ransom payment in exchange for the decryption key. Denial-of-service attacks are designed to overload a website or server with traffic, rendering it unavailable to users.

To protect against these types of cyber threats and attacks, organizations must take a proactive approach to cybersecurity. This includes implementing strong security controls, regularly monitoring systems for signs of compromise, and providing training to employees on how to recognize and respond to potential threats.

Cyber threat intelligence is an essential component of any cybersecurity strategy. This involves gathering and analyzing information about potential threats and attackers in order to better understand their motivations and tactics. By understanding the threat landscape, organizations can better prepare themselves to defend against attacks and minimize the impact of any security incidents.

In addition to implementing strong security controls and gathering threat intelligence, organizations must also comply with various cybersecurity regulations and standards. These regulations, such as the General Data Protection Regulation (GDPR) and the California Consumer Privacy Act (CCPA), are designed to protect individuals' data and privacy. Organizations that fail to comply with these regulations can face significant fines and reputational damage.

In conclusion, understanding cyber threats and attacks is essential for any organization that wants to protect itself from these risks. By implementing strong security controls, gathering threat intelligence, and complying with cybersecurity regulations, organizations can minimize the impact of potential security incidents and protect sensitive data and information.

Common types of cyber attacks

As technology continues to evolve, cyber attacks have become more sophisticated, and the number of attacks has increased. Hackers are always looking for new ways to exploit vulnerabilities in systems and networks, and it's essential to understand the different types of cyber attacks to protect yourself and your business.

Phishing Attacks:

Phishing is a type of social engineering attack where hackers send emails or messages that appear to be from a trusted source, such as a bank or a company you do business with. The goal is to trick you into clicking on a link or downloading an attachment that contains malware.

Ransomware:

Ransomware is a type of malware that encrypts your files and demands payment in exchange for the decryption key. These attacks can be devastating for businesses and individuals, as they can result in the loss of sensitive data or the complete shutdown of systems.

Malware:

Malware is a general term for any software that is designed to harm a computer system. This can include viruses, worms, and Trojan horses, which can be used to steal data, take control of systems, or cause damage to hardware.

Man-in-the-middle:

A Man-in-the-middle (MITM) attack occurs when a hacker intercepts communications between two parties, such as a user and a website or a user and a server. The goal is to steal data or modify the communication in some way without the user or the server being aware of the attack.

Denial-of-Service:

Denial-of-Service (DoS) attacks are designed to overwhelm a system or network with traffic, making it impossible for legitimate users to access the system or network. These attacks are often carried out using botnets, which are networks of compromised computers that are controlled by the attacker.

In conclusion, understanding the different types of cyber attacks is essential for protecting yourself and your business. By staying vigilant and taking steps to secure your systems and networks, you can reduce the risk of falling victim to these attacks and keep your data safe.

The cost of cyber attacks

The cost of cyber attacks has been increasing over the years and it is becoming a major concern for businesses and organizations. Cyber attacks can result in loss of sensitive data, financial loss, damage to reputation, and disruption of operations. With the increasing dependence on technology, the risk of cyber attacks is also increasing, making it important for businesses to invest in cybersecurity.

The financial cost of cyber attacks is significant. According to a report by Accenture, the average cost of cybercrime for an organization increased by 11% in 2019, reaching $13.0 million per organization. The cost of cyber attacks varies depending on the size of the organization, the type of attack, and the level of damage caused. Small businesses are particularly vulnerable as they may not have the resources to recover from a cyber attack.

In addition to financial costs, cyber attacks can also result in damage to reputation. Businesses that suffer a cyber attack may lose the trust of their customers and stakeholders. A survey by Ping Identity found that 78% of consumers would stop engaging with a brand online if it suffered a data breach. This loss of trust can have long-term consequences for the business.

Cyber attacks also have the potential to disrupt operations. A ransomware attack, for example, can lock a business out of its own systems, preventing it from carrying out its operations. This can have significant financial and reputational impacts.

In addition to the direct costs of cyber attacks, businesses may also face regulatory fines and legal action. Many countries have introduced data protection regulations, such as the General Data Protection Regulation (GDPR) in the European Union. Failure to comply with these regulations can result in significant fines and legal action.

Overall, the cost of cyber attacks is significant and can have long-term consequences for businesses. It is important for businesses to invest in cybersecurity to protect themselves from these risks. This investment can include measures such as employee training, regular security assessments, and the use of advanced security technologies. By taking these steps, businesses can reduce the risk of cyber attacks and protect themselves from the financial, reputational, and operational impacts of these attacks.

The importance of cybersecurity culture

The importance of cybersecurity culture cannot be overstated in today's digital age. Every organization, irrespective of its size or industry, must develop a cybersecurity culture that is ingrained in the company's DNA. This culture is essential to ensure that everyone in the organization is aware of the potential threats and takes necessary steps to prevent them.

The cybersecurity culture must start from the top and trickle down to every employee in the organization. The leadership team must set an example by making cybersecurity a priority and providing the necessary resources to develop and implement effective cybersecurity policies and practices. This includes investing in security technologies, conducting regular training programs, and creating a system to monitor and respond to security incidents.

Employees must also be educated on the importance of cybersecurity and the risks associated with a cyberattack. They must be trained on how to identify and report security incidents and how to respond to them. Employees should also be encouraged to report any suspicious activity or vulnerabilities to the IT department.

A strong cybersecurity culture also involves regularly testing the organization's security measures and processes. This includes conducting penetration testing, vulnerability assessments, and incident response drills to ensure that the organization is prepared to respond to a cyberattack.

In addition to protecting the organization's data and systems, a cybersecurity culture also helps to build trust with customers and partners. Customers are more likely to trust an organization that takes cybersecurity seriously and protects their data from potential breaches.

Finally, a cybersecurity culture is essential to comply with regulatory requirements. With the increase in data protection regulations such as GDPR, CCPA, and HIPAA, organizations must ensure that they are compliant with these regulations to avoid hefty fines and reputational damage.

In conclusion, a strong cybersecurity culture is essential for every organization to protect its data, systems, and reputation. It is crucial that organizations invest in cybersecurity training, technologies, and policies to create a culture of vigilance and safeguard against potential cyber threats.

Chapter 3: The Cybersecurity Mindset

The importance of cultivating a cybersecurity mindset

The importance of cultivating a cybersecurity mindset has never been more critical than it is today. The world is becoming more interconnected, and the digital landscape is expanding at an unprecedented rate. With this growth comes an increase in cyber threats, which can have damaging effects on individuals, organizations, and the world economy.

A cybersecurity mindset is a way of thinking that prioritizes the protection of digital assets against cyber threats. It involves being aware of potential risks, staying up to date with the latest threats and vulnerabilities, and taking proactive measures to prevent attacks.

For organizations, cultivating a cybersecurity mindset is essential to protect sensitive data, prevent financial losses, and maintain the trust of customers and stakeholders. It involves creating a culture of vigilance where everyone from the CEO to the entry-level employee understands the importance of cybersecurity and takes responsibility for protecting the company's digital assets.

Data privacy and protection are also critical aspects of a cybersecurity mindset. As individuals, we must be mindful of the information we share online and take steps to protect our personal data from cybercriminals. We must also demand that organizations we interact with prioritize data privacy and protection to ensure our information is not compromised.

Cyber threat intelligence is another vital aspect of a cybersecurity mindset. This involves staying up to date with the latest threats and vulnerabilities, analyzing data to identify potential risks, and taking proactive measures to prevent attacks before they occur.

In addition to being proactive, cybersecurity compliance and regulation are essential components of a cybersecurity mindset. Compliance with industry regulations and standards helps organizations ensure they are taking the necessary steps to protect their digital assets. Compliance also helps organizations avoid costly fines and reputational damage.

In conclusion, cultivating a cybersecurity mindset is critical in today's digital landscape. It involves being aware of potential risks, staying up to date with the latest threats and vulnerabilities, and taking proactive measures to prevent attacks. For organizations, a culture of vigilance is essential to protect sensitive data, prevent financial losses, and maintain the trust of customers and stakeholders. As individuals, we must also prioritize data privacy and protection and demand that organizations we interact with do the same. Finally, cybersecurity compliance and regulation are important components of a cybersecurity mindset, helping organizations ensure they are taking the necessary steps to protect their digital assets.

Understanding the psychology of cyber attackers

Understanding the psychology of cyber attackers is crucial for developing effective cybersecurity strategies. Cyber attackers can be individuals or groups with different motives and goals, but they all share common psychological traits that make them successful in their attacks. In this subchapter, we will explore the psychology of cyber attackers and how to counter their tactics.

One of the most common motives for cyber attackers is financial gain. Cybercriminals can use various tactics, such as phishing, malware, and ransomware, to steal money from individuals and organizations. These attackers are usually motivated by greed and the desire to make a quick profit. They often target vulnerable individuals and businesses that lack proper cybersecurity measures.

Another motive for cyber attackers is political or ideological reasons. These attackers may belong to a group or have a personal agenda that they want to promote. They can use their skills to launch attacks on government agencies, political parties, or businesses that they perceive as a threat to their beliefs. These attackers can be difficult to track down because they often hide behind anonymous online identities.

Some cyber attackers are motivated by revenge or personal gain. They may have a grudge against a particular individual or organization and use their skills to launch attacks to cause damage or embarrassment. These attackers can be particularly dangerous because they may have inside knowledge of the target's vulnerabilities and weaknesses.

Understanding the psychology of cyber attackers is essential for developing effective cybersecurity strategies. By understanding their motives and tactics, organizations can develop effective countermeasures to protect against attacks. This includes implementing robust cybersecurity policies and procedures, providing cybersecurity training to employees, and investing in the latest security technologies.

In conclusion, cyber attackers are a diverse group with different motives and goals. They can be motivated by financial gain, political or ideological reasons, or revenge. Understanding their psychology is critical for developing effective cybersecurity strategies to protect against attacks. By investing in the latest security technologies, providing cybersecurity training to employees, and implementing robust cybersecurity policies and procedures, organizations can minimize the risk of cyber attacks and protect their sensitive data.

Steps to develop a cybersecurity culture in the workplace

In today's digital age, cybersecurity has become a critical concern for businesses of all sizes. Cyber attacks are becoming more frequent, and the consequences of a security breach can be devastating. Therefore, it is essential for companies to develop a cybersecurity culture in the workplace to protect themselves and their customers' data.

Here are some steps businesses can take to develop a cybersecurity culture in the workplace:

1. Educate employees: The first step to developing a cybersecurity culture is educating employees about the importance of cybersecurity and the risks associated with cyber attacks. Employees should be trained on how to identify and respond to cyber threats, as well as the company's policies and procedures for handling sensitive data.

2. Implement strong security measures: Businesses should implement strong security measures such as firewalls, antivirus software, and encryption to protect their systems and data. Regular security updates and patches should also be installed to keep systems up-to-date and secure.

3. Develop a cybersecurity plan: A cybersecurity plan outlines how a company will protect itself from cyber threats and how it will respond in the event of a security breach. The plan should be regularly reviewed and updated to ensure it is effective and up-to-date.

4. Encourage reporting: Employees should be encouraged to report any suspicious activity or potential security breaches immediately. This will allow the company to respond quickly and minimize the damage caused by a security breach.

5. Conduct regular security audits: Regular security audits can help identify vulnerabilities in a company's systems and processes and ensure compliance with cybersecurity regulations and standards.

6. Foster a culture of vigilance: Finally, businesses should foster a culture of vigilance where everyone is responsible for cybersecurity. This means employees should be encouraged to be proactive in identifying and reporting potential security risks, and cybersecurity should be a top priority for everyone in the organization.

In conclusion, developing a cybersecurity culture in the workplace is essential for businesses to protect themselves and their customers' data. By educating employees, implementing strong security measures, developing a cybersecurity plan, encouraging reporting, conducting regular security audits, and fostering a culture of vigilance, businesses can improve their cybersecurity posture and reduce the risk of a security breach.

Integrating cybersecurity into business strategy

Integrating cybersecurity into business strategy is no longer an option but a necessity. With the increasing frequency and sophistication of cyberattacks, organizations can no longer afford to treat cybersecurity as an afterthought. Instead, it must be an integral part of the business strategy, just like finance, marketing, and operations.

The first step towards integrating cybersecurity into business strategy is to understand the risks and threats facing the organization. This involves conducting a risk assessment that identifies the organization's assets, the potential threats to those assets, and the vulnerabilities that could be exploited by attackers. Once the risks have been identified, the organization can develop a cybersecurity strategy that aligns with its overall business objectives.

One of the key aspects of integrating cybersecurity into business strategy is to ensure that cybersecurity is not seen as a separate function but an integral part of the business processes. This means that cybersecurity must be integrated into the development of new products and services, the design of business processes, and the selection of technology solutions. This can be achieved by involving cybersecurity experts in the decision-making process and ensuring that cybersecurity requirements are included in the procurement process.

Another important aspect of integrating cybersecurity into business strategy is to ensure that cybersecurity is not seen as a barrier to innovation. Too often, cybersecurity is seen as a hindrance to innovation, and this can lead to the adoption of insecure solutions. By integrating cybersecurity into the innovation process, organizations can ensure that innovative solutions are secure by design.

Finally, integrating cybersecurity into business strategy requires a cultural shift. Cybersecurity is not just the responsibility of the IT department but the responsibility of everyone in the organization. This means that cybersecurity awareness and training must be provided to all employees, and cybersecurity must be included in the performance metrics of all employees.

In conclusion, integrating cybersecurity into business strategy is essential for organizations that want to protect their assets, maintain customer trust, and comply with regulatory requirements. By treating cybersecurity as an integral part of the business strategy, organizations can ensure that cybersecurity is not an afterthought but a core component of their operations.

Chapter 4: Data Privacy and Protection

Understanding data privacy and protection

Understanding data privacy and protection

Data privacy and protection are crucial components of modern cybersecurity. Data is the lifeblood of the digital age, and the collection, storage, and use of this information has become a critical business function. However, data breaches and cyber threats pose a significant risk to businesses that rely on data. In this chapter, we will discuss what data privacy and protection are, why they are essential, and what businesses can do to ensure their data is secure.

What is data privacy?

Data privacy refers to the protection of personal information that is collected, stored, and processed by businesses. This includes information such as names, addresses, phone numbers, email addresses, and social security numbers. It also includes sensitive data such as financial information, medical records, and other personally identifiable information.

Why is data privacy important?

Data privacy is essential for several reasons. First, it is a legal requirement in many jurisdictions, and non-compliance can result in significant fines and legal action. Second, it is critical for protecting the privacy and security of individuals' personal information. Third, it helps businesses maintain customer trust and loyalty by demonstrating their commitment to protecting their customers' data.

What is data protection?

Data protection refers to the measures taken to secure data against unauthorized access, use, or loss. This includes physical security measures, such as locks and access controls, as well as technical measures, such as encryption and firewalls. Data protection is crucial for preventing data breaches and cyber attacks.

Why is data protection important?

Data protection is essential for several reasons. First, it helps prevent data breaches and cyber attacks, which can result in significant financial losses and damage to a company's reputation. Second, it is a legal requirement in many jurisdictions, and non-compliance can result in significant fines and legal action. Third, it helps businesses maintain customer trust and loyalty by demonstrating their commitment to protecting their customers' data.

What can businesses do to ensure data privacy and protection?

Businesses can take several steps to ensure data privacy and protection. First, they should develop clear data privacy policies and procedures and ensure that all employees are trained on these policies. Second, they should implement technical measures such as encryption and firewalls to protect data from unauthorized access. Third, they should regularly audit and monitor their systems for potential vulnerabilities and take steps to address any issues that are identified.

Conclusion

Data privacy and protection are critical components of modern cybersecurity. Businesses must take steps to ensure that their data is secure and protected from unauthorized access, use, or loss. By developing clear data privacy policies and procedures, implementing technical measures, and regularly auditing and monitoring their systems, businesses can protect themselves and their customers from data breaches and cyber attacks.

The importance of data privacy regulations

In today's digital age, data is considered the most valuable asset for businesses. However, with great data comes great responsibility. The importance of data privacy regulations cannot be stressed enough. These regulations not only protect the personal information of individuals but also ensure that businesses uphold ethical standards while collecting, processing, and storing data.

From the General Data Protection Regulation (GDPR) in Europe to the California Consumer Privacy Act (CCPA) in the United States, data privacy regulations are becoming increasingly stringent. Failure to comply with these regulations can result in severe penalties, including hefty fines and damage to a company's reputation.

Apart from regulatory compliance, data privacy regulations also promote transparency and trust between businesses and their customers. By implementing strong data privacy policies, businesses can assure their customers that their information is safe and secure.

Moreover, data privacy regulations play a crucial role in safeguarding against cyber threats. With cybercriminals constantly on the prowl, businesses must take every possible measure to protect their data. Regulations such as GDPR require businesses to report data breaches within 72 hours. This prompt reporting ensures that necessary action is taken to mitigate the damage caused by the breach.

In conclusion, data privacy regulations are essential for businesses to protect their customers' personal information, uphold ethical standards, and safeguard against cyber threats. Businesses must not only comply with these regulations but also prioritize data privacy and protection to build trust with their customers and ensure a secure digital future.

Best practices for protecting sensitive data

The Cybersecurity Mindset: Cultivating a Culture of Vigilance

In today's digital age, sensitive data is the lifeblood of businesses across the globe. From financial records to trade secrets, sensitive data is the critical ingredient that powers the modern economy. However, with the increase in cyber threats, it is now more important than ever for organizations to adopt best practices for protecting sensitive data.

One of the most important ways to protect sensitive data is to limit access to it. It is essential to ensure that only authorized individuals have access to sensitive data. This can be achieved by implementing access controls, such as password protection or multi-factor authentication. Organizations should also monitor access to sensitive data and identify any unauthorized access attempts.

Another important best practice for protecting sensitive data is encryption. Encryption is the process of converting sensitive data into a code that cannot be deciphered without the correct key. This is an effective way to protect data in transit or at rest. Encryption can be implemented at various levels, including the device level, the application level, and the network level.

Data backup and recovery is also an important best practice for protecting sensitive data. Organizations should make regular backups of their data and store them in a secure location. This ensures that in the event of a data breach or other disaster, the organization can recover its data quickly and efficiently.

In addition to these best practices, organizations should also implement a comprehensive cybersecurity strategy. This includes conducting regular risk assessments, implementing security policies and procedures, and training employees on cybersecurity best practices. Organizations should also stay up-to-date on the latest cyber threats and vulnerabilities and take appropriate measures to mitigate them.

Overall, protecting sensitive data is essential for the success of businesses in today's digital age. By adopting best practices such as limiting access, encrypting data, and implementing a comprehensive cybersecurity strategy, organizations can minimize the risk of data breaches and ensure the safety and security of their sensitive data.

Tools and technologies for data protection

In today's world, data protection should be a top priority for businesses. Data breaches not only have the potential to expose sensitive information, but they can also cause significant reputational and financial damage to an organization. Fortunately, there are several tools and technologies available to help protect against cyber threats and ensure data privacy and protection.

One of the most important tools for data protection is encryption. Encryption involves converting data into a code that is unreadable without a decryption key. This means that even if a hacker gains access to the data, they won't be able to read it without the key. Many modern encryption algorithms are virtually unbreakable, making them an effective way to protect data.

Another critical tool for data protection is firewalls. Firewalls are software or hardware systems that monitor incoming and outgoing network traffic and block any unauthorized access. They act as a barrier between the internal network and the outside world, preventing hackers from gaining access to sensitive data.

Antivirus software is another essential tool for data protection. It scans for and removes any malicious software that could compromise data security. Antivirus software is particularly important for businesses that use a lot of different devices, as it can protect against malware that may be introduced through various endpoints.

In addition to these tools, there are several technologies that can help with data protection. One such technology is identity and access management (IAM). IAM systems manage user access to data and applications, ensuring that only authorized users can access sensitive information. This not only helps to protect data but also helps to ensure compliance with data protection regulations such as GDPR.

Another important technology for data protection is data loss prevention (DLP). DLP systems monitor network traffic and endpoint activity to identify and prevent sensitive data from leaving the organization. This can help prevent data breaches caused by employees unintentionally or maliciously leaking sensitive information.

In conclusion, there are many tools and technologies available to help protect against cyber threats and ensure data privacy and protection. By implementing a combination of these tools, businesses can significantly reduce the risk of data breaches and protect their sensitive information.

Chapter 5: Cyber Threat Intelligence

Understanding cyber threat intelligence

Understanding Cyber Threat Intelligence

Cyber threat intelligence (CTI) is the process of collecting, analyzing, and disseminating information about potential cyber threats. It helps organizations to identify and understand the tactics, techniques, and procedures (TTPs) used by threat actors to target their networks, systems, and data. CTI also enables organizations to proactively detect, prevent, and respond to cyber attacks.

CTI is an essential component of any effective cybersecurity strategy. It enables organizations to stay ahead of cyber threats by providing timely and relevant information about potential threats. CTI also helps organizations to prioritize their cybersecurity efforts and allocate resources effectively.

There are two primary sources of CTI: internal and external. Internal CTI is based on data collected from an organization's own networks, systems, and applications. This includes information about network traffic, system logs, and user activity. External CTI, on the other hand, is based on data collected from external sources such as threat intelligence feeds, open-source intelligence (OSINT), and dark web monitoring.

CTI is not just about collecting data. It also involves analyzing and contextualizing that data to identify potential threats and vulnerabilities. This requires a combination of technical expertise and knowledge of the threat landscape. CTI analysts need to be able to identify patterns and anomalies in data, and understand the motivations and capabilities of threat actors.

CTI can help organizations to:

- Identify potential threats before they become a reality

- Prioritize cybersecurity efforts and allocate resources effectively

- Improve incident response times and reduce the impact of cyber attacks

- Stay up-to-date with the latest cyber threats and trends

- Meet regulatory compliance requirements

In conclusion, cyber threat intelligence is an essential component of any effective cybersecurity strategy. It enables organizations to stay ahead of cyber threats by providing timely and relevant information about potential threats. CTI analysts need to be able to collect, analyze, and contextualize data to identify potential threats and vulnerabilities. Organizations that invest in CTI can improve their cybersecurity posture and reduce the risk of cyber attacks.

The importance of threat intelligence in cybersecurity

The importance of threat intelligence in cybersecurity cannot be overstated. In today's digital landscape, cyber threats are becoming increasingly sophisticated and frequent. The only way to stay ahead of these threats is by having a well-informed and proactive approach to cybersecurity.

At its core, threat intelligence is the practice of gathering and analyzing information about potential cyber threats. This information can come from a variety of sources, including open-source intelligence, dark web monitoring, and even human intelligence. The goal of threat intelligence is to provide organizations with actionable insights that can help them identify, prevent, and respond to cyber threats.

One of the key benefits of threat intelligence is that it helps organizations stay ahead of the curve. By gathering information about emerging threats and vulnerabilities, organizations can take proactive measures to mitigate these risks before they become a problem. This can include implementing new security controls, patching vulnerabilities, and even changing business processes to reduce risk.

Another benefit of threat intelligence is that it enables organizations to better understand the threat landscape. By analyzing trends and patterns in cyber attacks, organizations can gain a deeper understanding of the tactics and techniques used by cyber criminals. This can help inform security strategies and help organizations better prepare for future attacks.

Threat intelligence is also essential for compliance and regulation. Many regulatory frameworks, such as GDPR and PCI DSS, require organizations to have a robust approach to cybersecurity. By leveraging threat intelligence, organizations can demonstrate to auditors and regulators that they are taking a proactive approach to cybersecurity and are actively working to protect sensitive data.

In conclusion, threat intelligence is a critical component of any cybersecurity strategy. By gathering and analyzing information about potential threats, organizations can stay ahead of the curve, better understand the threat landscape, and demonstrate compliance with regulatory frameworks. As cyber threats continue to evolve, threat intelligence will become increasingly important for organizations looking to stay ahead of the curve and protect their sensitive data.

How to collect and analyze threat intelligence

In today's world, cyber threats have become a ubiquitous concern for businesses and organizations. In order to protect themselves from these threats, it is essential for organizations to collect and analyze threat intelligence. Threat intelligence is the information that is used to identify and understand the potential cyber threats that an organization may face. In this subchapter, we will discuss how to collect and analyze threat intelligence.

The first step in collecting threat intelligence is to identify the sources of intelligence. These sources can be internal or external. Internal sources include logs, reports, and alerts generated by the organization's security tools. External sources include open-source intelligence, threat feeds, and information sharing groups.

Once the sources of intelligence are identified, it is important to ensure that the data collected is relevant and accurate. The data should be analyzed to identify patterns and trends, which can help to identify potential threats. This analysis can be done manually or using automated tools.

One of the most important aspects of collecting and analyzing threat intelligence is to ensure that the data is shared within the organization. This can help to ensure that all stakeholders are aware of potential threats and can take appropriate action. It is also important to share threat intelligence with external partners, such as law enforcement agencies, to ensure that they are aware of potential cyber threats.

In order to effectively collect and analyze threat intelligence, it is important to have a well-defined process in place. This process should outline the steps involved in collecting and analyzing data, as well as the roles and responsibilities of each member of the team. It should also include guidelines for sharing information and responding to potential threats.

In conclusion, collecting and analyzing threat intelligence is an essential part of any organization's cybersecurity strategy. By identifying potential threats and taking appropriate action, organizations can protect themselves from cyber attacks and ensure the safety of their data and assets.

Tools and technologies for threat intelligence

Tools and technologies for threat intelligence have become essential for businesses, organizations, and governments to detect and prevent cyber threats effectively. With the rise of cybercrime, it has become critical to have a proactive approach to cybersecurity, and threat intelligence is an essential component of that approach.

There are several tools and technologies available that can assist in the collection, analysis, and dissemination of threat intelligence. One of the most significant technologies in this regard is artificial intelligence (AI). AI can help in the identification of patterns and anomalies that may indicate a cyber threat. It can also assist in the automation of threat detection and response, making it easier for cybersecurity professionals to stay ahead of potential threats.

Another tool that is gaining popularity in the field of threat intelligence is machine learning. Machine learning algorithms can help in predicting threats by analyzing large amounts of data and identifying patterns that may indicate malicious activity. This technology can also assist in identifying the source of the threat, which can help in tracking down the attackers.

Other tools and technologies that are useful in threat intelligence include intrusion detection and prevention systems (IDPS), security information and event management (SIEM) systems, and threat intelligence platforms (TIPs). IDPS can detect and prevent unauthorized access to a network, while SIEM systems can collect and analyze security-related data from various sources to detect potential threats. TIPs, on the other hand, can help in the aggregation, analysis, and dissemination of threat intelligence, making it easier for organizations to stay informed about potential threats.

In addition to these tools and technologies, it is also essential to have a robust threat intelligence program in place. This program should include a clear understanding of the threat landscape, regular assessments of potential threats, and a plan for responding to incidents. It should also include regular training for employees on how to identify and report potential threats.

Overall, the tools and technologies for threat intelligence are critical for businesses, organizations, and governments to stay ahead of potential cyber threats. With the right tools and technologies, combined with a proactive approach to cybersecurity, organizations can minimize the risk of cyber attacks and protect their valuable data.

Chapter 6: Cybersecurity Compliance and Regulation

Understanding cybersecurity compliance and regulation

Understanding Cybersecurity Compliance and Regulation

In today's digital age, cybersecurity has become a critical issue for companies around the world. The increasing number of cyber attacks has led to the development of cybersecurity laws and regulations that aim to protect individuals and organizations from cyber threats. Understanding cybersecurity compliance and regulation is essential for organizations to protect themselves and their customers from cyber threats.

Cybersecurity compliance refers to the adherence to cybersecurity laws and regulations by organizations. These laws and regulations are designed to ensure that organizations take appropriate measures to protect their data and systems from cyber threats. Failure to comply with these regulations can result in fines, legal action, and damage to the organization's reputation.

One of the most important cybersecurity regulations is the General Data Protection Regulation (GDPR), which was introduced by the European Union in 2018. The GDPR aims to protect the privacy and data of EU citizens and requires organizations to take appropriate measures to protect personal data. Failure to comply with the GDPR can result in fines of up to 4% of the organization's global revenue.

Other important cybersecurity regulations include the Cybersecurity Information Sharing Act (CISA) and the Health Insurance Portability and Accountability Act (HIPAA) in the United States. CISA aims to improve cybersecurity by facilitating the sharing of cyber threat information between organizations and the government. HIPAA, on the other hand, aims to protect the privacy and security of individuals' health information.

To comply with cybersecurity regulations, organizations must implement appropriate cybersecurity measures and policies. This includes regular security assessments, employee training, and the use of encryption and other cybersecurity technologies. Organizations must also ensure that they have appropriate incident response plans in place to respond to cyber attacks.

In conclusion, understanding cybersecurity compliance and regulation is essential for organizations to protect themselves and their customers from cyber threats. Organizations must comply with cybersecurity regulations and implement appropriate cybersecurity measures and policies to ensure the security of their data and systems. Failure to comply with cybersecurity regulations can result in fines, legal action, and damage to the organization's reputation.

Overview of cybersecurity regulations around the world

In today's digital age, cybersecurity has become increasingly important to ensure the safety and protection of sensitive information. With the rise of cyber threats and attacks, many countries around the world have implemented cybersecurity regulations to ensure that companies and individuals are taking the necessary precautions to protect themselves and their data.

One of the most well-known cybersecurity regulations is the General Data Protection Regulation (GDPR) implemented by the European Union (EU) in 2018. The GDPR is designed to protect the personal data of EU citizens and ensure that companies are transparent about how they collect, use, and store this data. Failure to comply with the GDPR can result in hefty fines and legal action.

In the United States, the Federal Trade Commission (FTC) has implemented cybersecurity regulations for companies that handle personal information. The FTC requires companies to have a comprehensive security plan in place to protect this information and to notify affected individuals in the event of a data breach.

Other countries around the world have also implemented cybersecurity regulations to protect their citizens and their data. For example, Japan has implemented the Act on the Protection of Personal Information (APPI), while Australia has implemented the Privacy Act and the Notifiable Data Breaches (NDB) scheme.

It's worth noting that cybersecurity regulations can differ from country to country, and compliance can be complex. However, it's essential for companies to understand and comply with these regulations to avoid legal action, fines, and reputational damage.

In addition to complying with regulations, it's also important for companies to have a cybersecurity mindset and cultivate a culture of vigilance. This involves educating employees on cybersecurity best practices, regularly updating security measures, and staying up-to-date on the latest cyber threats and trends.

Overall, cybersecurity regulations around the world are designed to protect individuals and companies from cyber threats and attacks. It's essential for businesses to comply with these regulations and prioritize cybersecurity to ensure the safety and protection of their data and their customers.

Best practices for compliance and regulation

Best practices for compliance and regulation are critical in ensuring that businesses operate within the law and protect their customers' data. Cybersecurity compliance and regulations are constantly evolving, and it is crucial for businesses to stay up-to-date with these changes. Failure to comply with cybersecurity regulations can result in hefty fines, loss of customers, and damage to a company's reputation. In this subchapter, we will discuss some best practices for compliance and regulation that businesses can implement to protect their data and ensure compliance with the law.

Firstly, businesses should ensure they have a comprehensive understanding of the regulations that apply to their industry. Regulations such as the General Data Protection Regulation (GDPR) and the California Consumer Privacy Act (CCPA) have specific requirements that businesses must adhere to. It is essential to have a dedicated team responsible for monitoring and implementing these regulations.

Secondly, businesses should conduct regular risk assessments to identify potential vulnerabilities in their systems. Risk assessments should be conducted on a regular basis and should involve all stakeholders, including IT, legal, and compliance teams. This will help businesses identify potential threats and implement measures to mitigate them.

Thirdly, businesses should implement strong access controls to limit the number of people who have access to sensitive data. This can be achieved through identity and access management (IAM) systems, which control who can access specific data and systems. IAM systems also enable businesses to monitor user activity and detect any unusual behavior.

Fourthly, businesses should implement a data retention policy to ensure that data is not stored longer than necessary. This will help businesses comply with regulations that require them to delete data after a specific period.

Finally, businesses should invest in training and awareness programs to educate employees about cybersecurity regulations and best practices. Employees are the first line of defense against cyber threats, and they need to understand their role in protecting the company's data.

In conclusion, cybersecurity compliance and regulation are critical for businesses in today's digital world. Implementing best practices such as understanding regulations, conducting regular risk assessments, implementing access controls, implementing a data retention policy, and investing in training and awareness programs can help businesses protect their data and comply with the law.

Tools and technologies for compliance and regulation

In today's digital age, compliance and regulation are critical for businesses to maintain a secure and safe environment for their customers. The cyber threats are constantly evolving, and companies must keep up with the latest trends and technologies to ensure they are in compliance with the latest regulations.

The cybersecurity industry has been growing rapidly over the past few years, and with it, the tools and technologies to support compliance and regulation have also been expanding. Here are some of the key tools and technologies that businesses can use to ensure they are compliant with cybersecurity regulations:

1. Security Information and Event Management (SIEM) systems: These tools are designed to collect and analyze security events and logs from various sources in real-time. SIEM systems can help businesses detect and respond to security incidents promptly.

2. Data Loss Prevention (DLP) solutions: DLP solutions help businesses prevent data breaches by monitoring and controlling sensitive data. These solutions can identify and block unauthorized data access or transmission.

3. Identity and Access Management (IAM) systems: IAM systems help businesses manage user access to critical resources, ensuring that only authorized users can access sensitive data and applications.

4. Vulnerability scanning and management tools: These tools can help businesses discover vulnerabilities in their systems and applications, prioritize them based on their risk level, and provide guidance on how to address them.

5. Encryption technologies: Encryption technologies can help businesses protect their sensitive data by encrypting it at rest and in-transit. They can also secure communications channels, such as email, to prevent data leaks.

6. Compliance management software: Compliance management software can help businesses automate compliance workflows, track compliance status, and generate reports for auditors.

In conclusion, the use of these tools and technologies can help businesses stay compliant with cybersecurity regulations and protect their customers' data. It is crucial for businesses to stay up-to-date with the latest cybersecurity trends and technologies to ensure they are protected from cyber threats.

Chapter 7: The Future of Cybersecurity

Emerging cybersecurity trends

Emerging Cybersecurity Trends

In today's digital age, cybersecurity is an ever-evolving field. As businesses and individuals rely more on technology, the risks of cyber threats are increasing. Cybercriminals are becoming more sophisticated and are constantly finding new ways to exploit vulnerabilities. In this subchapter, we will discuss some of the emerging cybersecurity trends that businesses and individuals need to be aware of.

1. Artificial Intelligence (AI) and Machine Learning (ML)

AI and ML are transforming the cybersecurity landscape. They are being used to detect and respond to cyber threats in real-time. Machine learning algorithms can analyze vast amounts of data and identify patterns that are indicative of a cyber attack. This can help organizations to respond quickly and effectively to threats.

2. Internet of Things (IoT) Security

The proliferation of IoT devices is creating new cybersecurity challenges. These devices are often not designed with security in mind, making them vulnerable to attacks. As more devices connect to the internet, the risk of cyber attacks increases. Organizations need to ensure that their IoT devices are secure and that they are regularly updated with the latest security patches.

3. Cloud Security

As more businesses move their data and applications to the cloud, cloud security is becoming a critical issue. Cloud providers are responsible for the security of their infrastructure, but businesses are responsible for the security of their data and applications. This means that businesses need to ensure that they have appropriate security measures in place, such as encryption and access controls.

4. Quantum Computing

Quantum computing has the potential to revolutionize cybersecurity. It can break encryption algorithms that are currently considered secure. This means that organizations need to start thinking about post-quantum cryptography and developing new encryption methods that can withstand quantum attacks.

5. Cyber Insurance

As cyber threats become more prevalent, cyber insurance is becoming increasingly important. Cyber insurance policies can help businesses to recover from cyber attacks, including the costs associated with data breaches and business interruption. However, businesses need to ensure that they have appropriate security measures in place to reduce the risk of a cyber attack in the first place.

In conclusion, cybersecurity is a constantly evolving field, and businesses and individuals need to stay up-to-date with the latest trends and threats. By understanding these emerging cybersecurity trends, organizations can take proactive steps to protect themselves from cyber attacks and safeguard their sensitive data.

The impact of artificial intelligence and machine learning on cybersecurity

The impact of artificial intelligence and machine learning on cybersecurity is a topic of great interest in the technology and business world. With the growing number of cyber threats, organizations are turning to AI and machine learning to enhance their cybersecurity capabilities.

AI and machine learning can help organizations detect and prevent cyber attacks in real-time. These technologies can analyze large amounts of data and identify patterns that may indicate a potential threat. This allows organizations to respond quickly and effectively to cyber attacks, reducing the damage caused by these incidents.

One of the key benefits of AI and machine learning in cybersecurity is their ability to adapt to new threats. These technologies can learn from past incidents and use this knowledge to improve their detection and prevention capabilities. This means that organizations can stay one step ahead of cyber criminals, who are constantly developing new tactics and strategies to breach security systems.

However, AI and machine learning also pose a challenge for cybersecurity professionals. As these technologies become more sophisticated, cyber criminals are also finding new ways to exploit them. For example, hackers can use AI to create more convincing phishing emails or to evade detection by security systems.

To address these challenges, organizations must ensure that their cybersecurity strategies are up-to-date and include the latest technologies and techniques. They must also invest in training and education for their employees, who play a critical role in maintaining a strong cybersecurity posture.

In addition, cybersecurity compliance and regulation are becoming increasingly important in the age of AI and machine learning. Governments and regulatory bodies are introducing new laws and regulations to protect sensitive data and prevent cyber attacks. Organizations must ensure that they comply with these regulations to avoid costly fines and reputational damage.

In conclusion, the impact of artificial intelligence and machine learning on cybersecurity is both positive and negative. These technologies can enhance organizations' ability to detect and prevent cyber attacks, but they also pose new challenges and risks. By staying up-to-date with the latest cybersecurity trends and investing in training and education, organizations can mitigate these risks and maintain a strong cybersecurity posture.

The role of cybersecurity in digital transformation

The role of cybersecurity in digital transformation cannot be overemphasized. With the rapid advancement of technology and the increasing interconnectedness of devices, businesses are now faced with more sophisticated threats and vulnerabilities. Cybersecurity has become a critical aspect of digital transformation, as it ensures that the digital transformation journey is secure and resilient. In this subchapter, we will explore the role of cybersecurity in digital transformation and how it impacts businesses.

One of the key benefits of digital transformation is the ability to improve business processes, enhance customer experience, and increase efficiency. However, this transformation comes with risks, particularly cybersecurity risks. Cybersecurity is essential to protect against cyber threats, which are becoming more sophisticated, and the consequences of a successful cyber attack can be devastating. For example, a cyber attack can lead to data breaches, loss of intellectual property, financial loss, and reputational damage.

To mitigate these risks, cybersecurity must be integrated into the digital transformation journey from the onset. Cybersecurity should not be an afterthought, but rather a critical component of the transformation process. This means that cybersecurity should be considered at every stage of the digital transformation journey, from planning to implementation and beyond. It is essential to ensure that cybersecurity is an integral part of the organizational culture and that all employees understand their role in protecting the business from cyber threats.

Another critical aspect of cybersecurity in digital transformation is data privacy and protection. With the increasing amount of data being generated and stored, businesses must ensure that sensitive data is protected from unauthorized access, theft, or misuse. This is particularly important for regulated industries such as healthcare, finance, and government. Businesses must comply with data privacy regulations such as GDPR, HIPAA, and CCPA, which require them to implement appropriate security measures to protect sensitive data.

Cyber threat intelligence is another critical aspect of cybersecurity in digital transformation. Cyber threat intelligence involves gathering, analyzing, and sharing information about cyber threats to enable proactive threat detection and response. This information can be used to identify emerging threats and vulnerabilities, develop effective security controls, and improve incident response capabilities.

Finally, cybersecurity compliance and regulation play a vital role in digital transformation. Businesses must comply with various cybersecurity regulations such as PCI DSS, NIST, ISO 27001, and others. Compliance with these regulations is essential to ensure that businesses are implementing appropriate security measures to protect against cyber threats.

In conclusion, cybersecurity is a critical component of digital transformation. Businesses must ensure that cybersecurity is integrated into the digital transformation journey from the onset and that all employees understand their role in protecting the business from cyber threats. Data privacy and protection, cyber threat intelligence, and cybersecurity compliance and regulation are all critical aspects of cybersecurity in digital transformation. By adopting a cybersecurity mindset and cultivating a culture of vigilance, businesses can ensure that their digital transformation journey is secure and resilient.

Future challenges and opportunities in cybersecurity

The future of cybersecurity is both challenging and full of opportunities. As technology continues to advance, cyber threats are becoming more sophisticated and complex. Organizations across all industries are facing an ever-growing risk of cyber attacks, data breaches, and other malicious cyber activities. The rise of the internet of things (IoT), cloud computing, and artificial intelligence (AI) has further increased the attack surface for cybercriminals.

One of the biggest challenges in the future of cybersecurity is the shortage of skilled cybersecurity professionals. According to a report by Cybersecurity Ventures, there will be 3.5 million unfilled cybersecurity jobs by 2021. This talent gap poses a significant threat to organizations' ability to protect themselves from cyber attacks. Therefore, organizations need to invest in training and upskilling their employees to build a strong cybersecurity workforce.

Another challenge is the need to balance cybersecurity with privacy and data protection. With the increasing amount of personal data being collected, stored, and processed by organizations, there is a growing concern about how this data is being used and protected. Organizations need to ensure they are complying with data protection regulations such as GDPR, CCPA, and HIPAA. They also need to be transparent about their data collection and usage policies to build trust with their customers.

The future of cybersecurity also presents opportunities for innovation and growth. The use of AI and machine learning can help organizations detect and respond to cyber threats more effectively. Blockchain technology can provide secure and tamper-proof data storage and transfer. The adoption of zero-trust security models can help organizations build a more resilient cybersecurity posture.

To stay ahead of the curve, organizations need to adopt a proactive approach to cybersecurity. This means investing in threat intelligence and monitoring tools to detect and respond to cyber threats in real-time. They also need to prioritize cybersecurity in their business strategy and ensure it is integrated into all aspects of their operations.

In conclusion, the future of cybersecurity presents both challenges and opportunities. Organizations need to be proactive in addressing the talent gap, balancing cybersecurity with privacy and data protection, and adopting innovative security technologies. With the right mindset and strategy, organizations can build a strong cybersecurity culture and protect themselves from the ever-evolving cyber threat landscape.

Chapter 8: Conclusion

Summary of key takeaways

In "The Cybersecurity Mindset: Cultivating a Culture of Vigilance," author Neil Daswani provides a comprehensive guide for individuals and organizations to develop a proactive approach towards cybersecurity. The book is a must-read for anyone interested in technology and business, particularly those in the cybersecurity, data privacy and protection, cyber threat intelligence, and cybersecurity compliance and regulation niches.

The key takeaway from the book is that cybersecurity is not just a technical problem, but also a cultural one. It requires a mindset shift that emphasizes vigilance and proactive measures to prevent cyber-attacks. Daswani emphasizes the importance of creating a security-aware culture, where everyone in the organization understands the risks and takes responsibility for protecting sensitive data.

One of the most significant challenges facing organizations today is the growing sophistication of cyber-attacks. Daswani offers practical advice on how organizations can stay ahead of cybercriminals by adopting a more proactive approach to cybersecurity. He recommends implementing a threat intelligence program that leverages advanced analytics and machine learning algorithms to identify potential threats before they can cause damage.

Another key takeaway from the book is the importance of compliance and regulation in cybersecurity. Daswani stresses the need for organizations to comply with industry standards and regulations such as the General Data Protection Regulation (GDPR) and the Payment Card Industry Data Security Standard (PCI DSS). Failure to comply with these regulations can result in significant financial and reputational damage.

Finally, Daswani emphasizes the importance of privacy and data protection in cybersecurity. He recommends implementing a privacy-by-design approach, where privacy is considered at every stage of the development process. This approach ensures that sensitive data is protected from the outset, rather than being bolted on as an afterthought.

Overall, "The Cybersecurity Mindset: Cultivating a Culture of Vigilance" provides a comprehensive guide for individuals and organizations to develop a proactive approach towards cybersecurity. The book is a valuable resource for anyone interested in technology and business, particularly those in the cybersecurity, data privacy and protection, cyber threat intelligence, and cybersecurity compliance and regulation niches.

Final thoughts on cultivating a culture of vigilance

Final Thoughts on Cultivating a Culture of Vigilance

In today's digital age, cybersecurity should be at the forefront of every business and organization's priorities. Cyber threats are constantly evolving, and cybercriminals are becoming more sophisticated in their tactics. This means that cultivating a culture of vigilance is essential to staying ahead of the game and protecting your organization from cyber threats.

At the heart of a culture of vigilance is the idea that cybersecurity is everyone's responsibility. It's not just the IT department's job to keep the organization safe from cyber threats. Every employee, from the CEO down to the lowest level employee, has a role to play in protecting the organization's data and systems.

To cultivate a culture of vigilance, it's important to start with education and training. Employees need to be aware of the latest cyber threats and how to spot them. They also need to know how to respond if they suspect a cyber attack has occurred. Regular training sessions and workshops can help keep cybersecurity top of mind for employees.

Another important aspect of cultivating a culture of vigilance is creating a strong cybersecurity policy. This policy should outline the organization's approach to cybersecurity, including best practices for data protection and guidelines for using technology safely. The policy should also be regularly reviewed and updated to ensure it stays relevant and effective.

Compliance with cybersecurity regulations is also crucial for cultivating a culture of vigilance. Organizations need to be aware of the latest regulations and ensure they are in compliance. This not only helps protect the organization from potential fines and legal action, but it also shows a commitment to cybersecurity to employees, customers, and stakeholders.

Finally, a culture of vigilance requires ongoing monitoring and assessment. Cyber threats are constantly evolving, and organizations need to stay on top of the latest trends and vulnerabilities. Regular risk assessments and penetration testing can help identify areas of weakness and allow organizations to proactively address them.

In conclusion, cultivating a culture of vigilance is essential for protecting your organization from cyber threats. It requires education and training, a strong cybersecurity policy, compliance with regulations, and ongoing monitoring and assessment. By making cybersecurity a priority and involving every employee in the process, organizations can create a culture of vigilance that will help keep them safe in today's digital age.

Call to action for readers to take steps to improve their cybersecurity mindset.

In today's digital age, cybersecurity has become a critical concern for businesses and individuals alike. Cyber threats are evolving rapidly, and hackers are becoming more sophisticated in their techniques. Therefore, it's crucial for everyone to improve their cybersecurity mindset to protect themselves from cyber attacks.

Here are some steps you can take to improve your cybersecurity mindset:

1. Understand the risks: The first step to improving your cybersecurity mindset is to understand the risks. Cyber threats can come in many forms, from phishing emails to ransomware attacks. By understanding the risks, you can take steps to protect yourself from them.

2. Use strong passwords: Passwords are the first line of defense against cyber attacks. Use strong and unique passwords for all your accounts, and avoid using the same password for multiple accounts.

3. Keep your software up to date: Software updates often include security patches that fix vulnerabilities that hackers can exploit. Therefore, it's essential to keep your software up to date to ensure that you are protected from the latest threats.

4. Use two-factor authentication: Two-factor authentication adds an extra layer of security to your accounts. It requires you to provide two forms of authentication (such as a password and a code sent to your phone) to access your account.

5. Be wary of phishing emails: Phishing emails are designed to trick you into giving away your personal information. Be wary of emails that ask you to click on a link or provide personal information.

6. Backup your data: Backing up your data is essential in case of a ransomware attack or other data loss. Make sure to backup your data regularly and keep it in a secure location.

By following these steps, you can improve your cybersecurity mindset and protect yourself from cyber threats. Remember, cybersecurity is everyone's responsibility, so take the necessary steps to protect yourself and your business from cyber attacks.

The Cybersecurity Mindset: Cultivating a Culture of Vigilance